Money Math

★ Addition and Subtraction ★

by **David A. Adler** · illustrated by **Edward Miller**

Holiday House  New York

Betsy Ross
GIFT SHOP

Flags
$2.00

Postcards
$1.00

Let Freedom Ring!

MUGS
$5.00

Keychains

Magnets

Have you ever gone shopping? There's lots of math in shopping.
If you want to know how much you can spend, you need to count your money.

Counting money is money addition.

Before you count you need to know the **value** of each **bill** and **coin**.

The
dollar
is central to our money system.

I am Abraham Lincoln. I was the 16th U.S. president. My portrait is on the penny and the 5-dollar bill.

Each **penny**,

I am Thomas Jefferson. I was the 3rd U.S. president. My portrait is on the nickel. I wrote the Declaration of Independence.

nickel,

dime,

I am John F. Kennedy. I was the 35th U.S. president. My portrait is on the half-dollar. I encouraged America to travel to the moon.

I am Franklin D. Roosevelt. I was the 32nd U.S. president. My portrait is on the dime.

quarter,

and **half-dollar**

is a **fraction**, a part, of a dollar.

A **penny** is **1 cent**. The total value of **100 pennies** is **one dollar**.
Each penny is $\frac{1}{100}$ of a dollar.

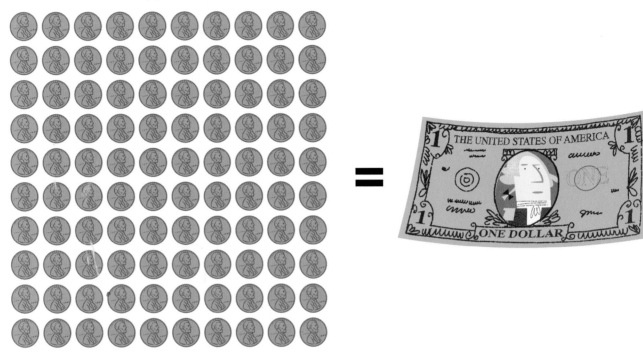

A **nickel** is **5 cents**. The total value of **20 nickels** is **one dollar**.
Each nickel is $\frac{5}{100}$ or $\frac{1}{20}$ of a dollar.

I will trade you 20 nickels for a dollar bill.

Sure!

A **dime** is **10 cents**. The total value of **10 dimes** is **one dollar**. Each dime is $\frac{10}{100}$ or $\frac{1}{10}$ of a dollar.

A **quarter** is **25 cents**. The total value of **4 quarters** is **one dollar**. Each quarter is $\frac{25}{100}$ or $\frac{1}{4}$ of a dollar.

A **half-dollar** is **50 cents**. The total value of **2 half-dollars** is **one dollar**. Each half-dollar is $\frac{50}{100}$ or $\frac{1}{2}$ of a dollar.

Do you have a dollar bill in exchange for 2 half-dollars?

Yes, I do.

What's the value of the coins below?
The easiest way to find the total value of
the coins is to count them in order. Begin with
the coin of greatest value. With these coins you
would first count the quarter. Next count the coin
with the second highest value, and so on.

I'm Alexander
Hamilton. I was the
1st Secretary of the
Treasury. My portrait
is on the
10-dollar bill.

Add the quarter
to the nickel, then add
the 3 pennies.

The value of the coins is 33¢.

The ¢ means **cents**.

50¢   **25¢**   **10¢**   **5¢**   **1¢**

The value of the coins is 72¢.

The value of the coins is 58¢.

What's the total value of these coins?

I am Benjamin Franklin. My portrait is on the 100-dollar bill. I was a founding father of the U.S. of America.

A penny saved is a penny earned!

The value of these coins is 142¢.

In general, when the amount of money is **100¢ or more**, the **¢** sign is no longer used. 142 cents is written $1.42.

The $ is a dollar sign.

decimal
point

$1.42

dollars

cents

The **dot** between the 1 and the 4 is a **decimal point**.

$1.42 is read "one dollar and forty-two cents."

The number to the left of the decimal point represents the dollars.

The number to the right represents the cents.

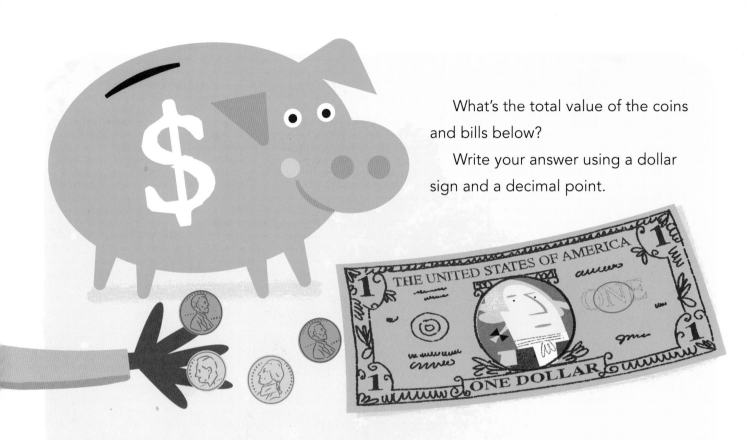

What's the total value of the coins and bills below?

Write your answer using a dollar sign and a decimal point.

What's the total value of the bills and coins below?

Write your answer using a dollar sign and a decimal point.

(Answers are on page 30.)

What's the total value of the coins and bills above?

Write your answer using a dollar sign and a decimal point.

(Answer is on page 30.)

You can have fun practicing coin addition. You can practice by solving coin puzzles.

Get lots of coins. Get half-dollars, quarters, dimes, nickels, and pennies. You'll need them to do money math.

A **quarter** is **25¢**.

How many other ways can you make 25¢?

Here are **11** ways to make **25¢**.

1 dime and 15 pennies are 25¢.

2 nickels and 15 pennies are 25¢.

1 nickel and 20 pennies are 25¢.

25 pennies are 25¢.

14

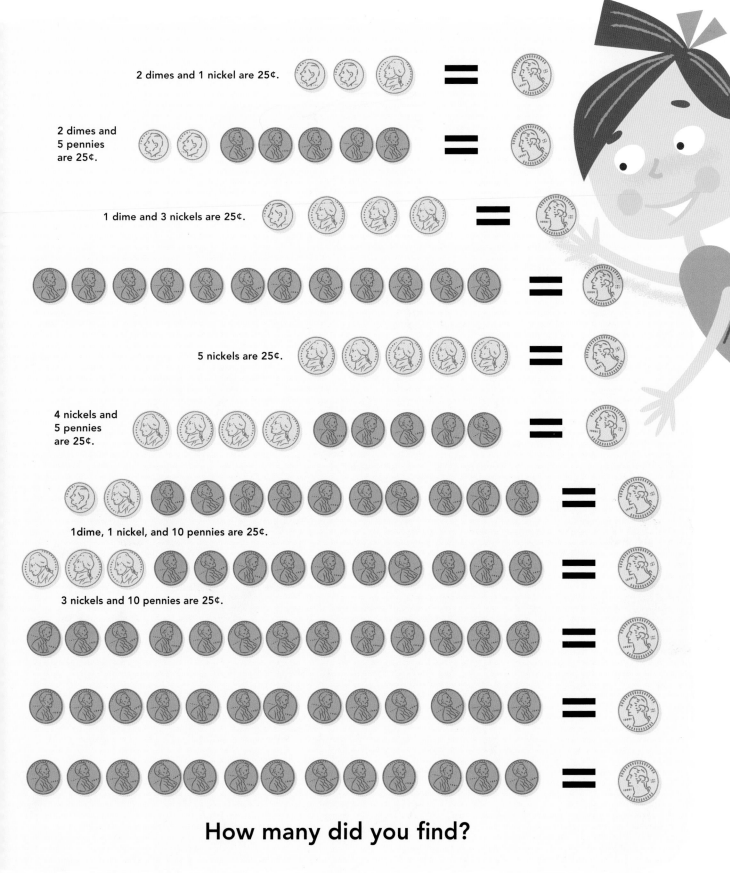

2 dimes and 1 nickel are 25¢. =

2 dimes and 5 pennies are 25¢. =

1 dime and 3 nickels are 25¢. =

=

5 nickels are 25¢. =

4 nickels and 5 pennies are 25¢. =

1 dime, 1 nickel, and 10 pennies are 25¢. =

3 nickels and 10 pennies are 25¢. =

=

=

How many did you find?

There are **24** different ways to make **35¢**.
Here are some of them.

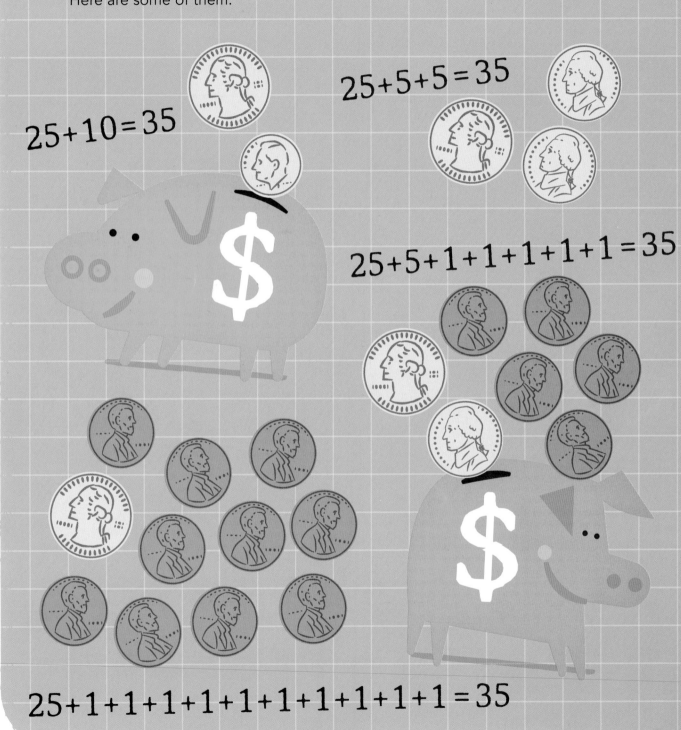

25 + 5 + 5 = 35

25 + 10 = 35

25 + 5 + 1 + 1 + 1 + 1 + 1 = 35

25 + 1 + 1 + 1 + 1 + 1 + 1 + 1 + 1 + 1 + 1 = 35

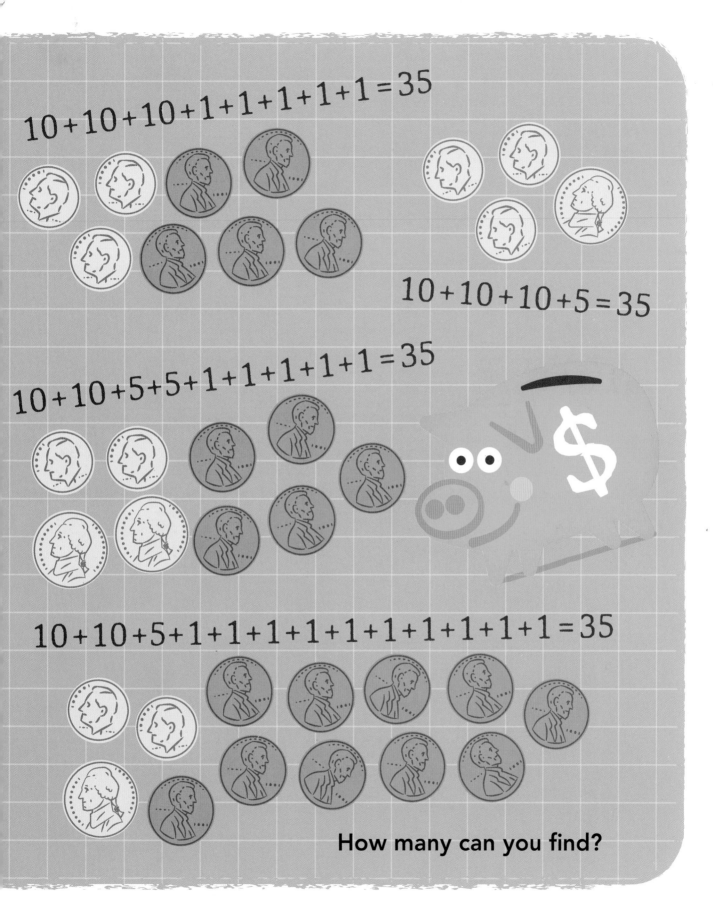

$10+10+10+1+1+1+1+1=35$

$10+10+10+5=35$

$10+10+5+5+1+1+1+1+1=35$

$10+10+5+1+1+1+1+1+1+1+1+1+1=35$

How many can you find?

(All 24 are listed on page 30.)

There are **50** different ways to make **50¢**.
Here are some of them.

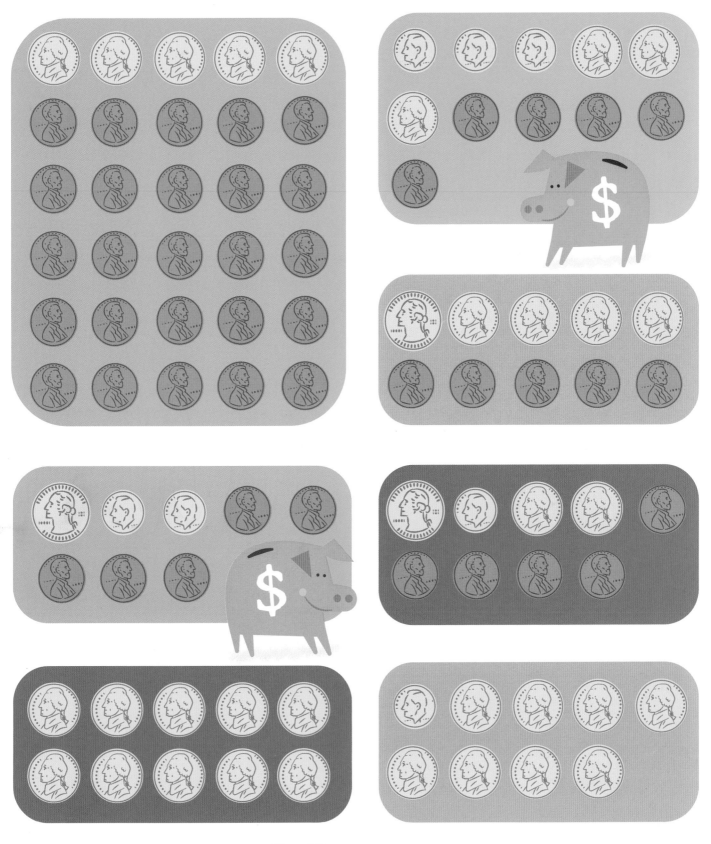

How many can you find?

(All 50 ways are listed on page 30.)

If you can count money you can use coins to help you practice **addition**.

Here's an addition problem:

27
+ 12
= ?

First do the problem as you would do any addition problem.

Receipt
27
+ 12
= 39

Now check your answer using money math.
Count out 27¢.
Count out 12¢.

Now put the coins together and find their total value.

27¢
+ 12¢
= 39¢

Here's another addition problem:

$$\begin{array}{r} 18 \\ + \ 34 \\ \hline = \ ? \end{array}$$

First do the problem as you would do any addition problem.

Now, check your answer using money math.
Count out 18¢.
Count out 34¢.

Memo
$$\begin{array}{r} 18 \\ + \ 34 \\ \hline = \ 52 \end{array}$$

Now put the coins together and find their total value.

$$\begin{array}{r} 18¢ \\ + \ 34¢ \\ \hline = \ 52¢ \end{array}$$

Here are some **addition problems**:

First do them as math problems. Then use money math to check your answers.

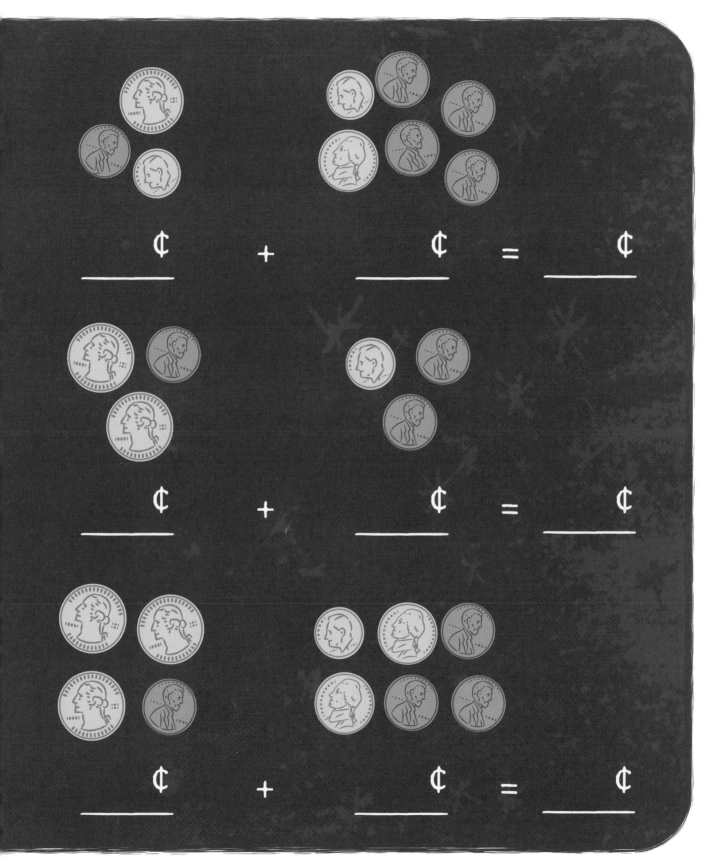

_____ ¢ + _____ ¢ = _____ ¢

_____ ¢ + _____ ¢ = _____ ¢

_____ ¢ + _____ ¢ = _____ ¢

(Answers are on page 31.)

Counting money is **money addition.**

Giving change is **money subtraction.**

Many times, when you shop, you don't pay exactly what an item costs. You pay extra. You expect the clerk to return the difference between what you paid and the cost of the item. You expect the clerk to give you **change**.

At a candy store, you might pay 3 quarters, 75¢, for a 59¢ chocolate bar. You paid more than 59¢, the cost of the chocolate bar. How much more? How much change should you get?

You could find the answer by **subtracting**.

$$75$$
$$- 59$$
$$= ?$$

You could also find the answer by using money math.

Begin with 75¢: 2 quarters, 1 dime, 2 nickels, and 5 pennies.

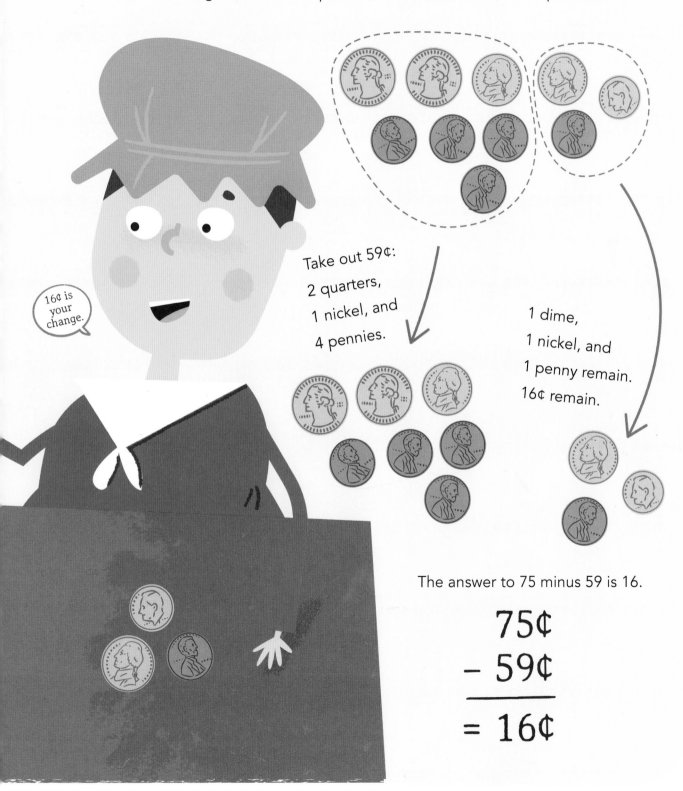

16¢ is your change.

Take out 59¢:
2 quarters,
1 nickel, and
4 pennies.

1 dime,
1 nickel, and
1 penny remain.
16¢ remain.

The answer to 75 minus 59 is 16.

$$75¢$$
$$-\ 59¢$$
$$=\ 16¢$$

Here are some **subtraction problems**:

For the first problem, 50 minus 29, begin with 1 quarter, 2 dimes, and 5 pennies.
Take out 29¢: 1 quarter and 4 pennies. How much money remains?

Here is 50¢.

Here is 50¢ with 29¢ taken out.

50¢
− 29¢
───
= ? ¢

73¢
− 67¢
───
= ? ¢

25¢
− 19¢
───
= ? ¢

25 − 19
equals?

For the second problem, 73 minus 67, begin with 2 quarters, 1 dime, 2 nickels, and 3 pennies. Take out 67¢: 2 quarters, 1 dime, 1 nickel, and 2 pennies. How much money remains?

Here is 73¢.

Here is 73¢ with 67¢ taken out.

For the third problem, 25 minus 19, begin with 1 dime, 2 nickels, and 5 pennies. Take out 19¢: 1 dime, 1 nickel, and 4 pennies. How much money remains?

Here is 25¢.

Here is 25¢ with 19¢ taken out.

(Answers are on page 31.)

Doing money math is fun.
Math should be fun.
Some people think going shopping
and spending coins and bills is fun.

28

Answers

p.12
$1.17
$2.97

p.13
$4.77

pp. 16–17
24 ways to make 35¢

1 quarter and 1 dime are 35¢
1 quarter and 2 nickels are 35¢
1 quarter and 1 nickel and 5 pennies are 35¢
1 quarter and 10 pennies are 35¢
3 dimes and 1 nickel are 35¢
3 dimes and 5 pennies are 25¢
2 dimes and 3 nickels are 35¢
2 dimes, 2 nickels, and 5 pennies are 35¢
2 dimes, 1 nickel, and 10 pennies are 35¢
2 dimes and 15 pennies are 35¢
1 dime and 5 nickels are 35¢
1 dime, 4 nickels, and 5 pennies are 35¢
1 dime, 3 nickels, and 10 pennies are 35¢
1 dime, 2 nickels, and 15 pennies are 35¢
1 dime, 1 nickel, and 20 pennies are 35¢
1 dime and 25 pennies are 35¢
7 nickels are 35¢
6 nickels and 5 pennies are 35¢
5 nickels and 10 pennies are 35¢
4 nickels and 15 pennies are 35¢
3 nickels and 20 pennies are 35¢
2 nickels and 25 pennies are 35¢
1 nickel and 30 pennies are 35¢
35 pennies are 35¢

pp. 18–19
50 ways to make 50¢

1 half-dollar is 50¢
2 quarters are 50¢
1 quarter, 2 dimes, and 1 nickel are 50¢
1 quarter, 2 dimes, and 5 pennies are 50¢
1 quarter, 1 dime, and 3 nickels are 50¢
1 quarter, 1 dime, 2 nickels, and
    5 pennies are 50¢
1 quarter, 1 dime, 1 nickel, and
    10 pennies are 50¢
1 quarter, 1 dime, and 15 pennies are 50¢
1 quarter and 5 nickels are 50¢
1 quarter, 4 nickels, and 5 pennies are 50¢
1 quarter, 3 nickels, and 10 pennies are 50¢
1 quarter, 2 nickels, and 15 pennies are 50¢
1 quarter, 1 nickel, and 20 pennies are 50¢
1 quarter and 25 pennies are 50¢
5 dimes are 50¢
4 dimes and 2 nickels are 50¢
4 dimes, 1 nickel, and 5 pennies are 50¢
4 dimes and 10 pennies are 50¢
3 dimes and 4 nickels are 50¢
3 dimes, 3 nickels, and 5 pennies are 50¢
3 dimes, 2 nickels, and 10 pennies are 50¢
3 dimes, 1 nickel, and 15 pennies are 50¢
3 dimes and 20 pennies are 50¢
2 dimes and 6 nickels are 50¢
2 dimes, 5 nickels, and 5 pennies are 50¢
2 dimes, 4 nickels, and 10 pennies are 50¢
2 dimes, 3 nickels, and 15 pennies are 50¢
2 dimes, 2 nickels, and 20 pennies are 50¢
2 dimes, 1 nickel, and 25 pennies are 50¢
2 dimes and 30 pennies are 50¢
1 dime and 8 nickels are 50¢
1 dime, 7 nickels, and 5 pennies are 50¢
1 dime, 6 nickels, and 10 pennies are 50¢
1 dime, 5 nickels, and 15 pennies are 50¢
1 dime, 4 nickels, and 20 pennies are 50¢
1 dime, 3 nickels, and 25 pennies are 50¢
1 dime, 2 nickels, and 30 pennies are 50¢
1 dime, 1 nickel, and 35 pennies are 50¢

1 dime and 40 pennies are 50¢
10 nickels are 50¢
9 nickels and 5 pennies are 50¢
8 nickels and 10 pennies are 50¢
7 nickels and 15 pennies are 50¢
6 nickels and 20 pennies are 50¢
5 nickels and 25 pennies are 50¢
4 nickels and 30 pennies are 50¢
3 nickels and 35 pennies are 50¢
2 nickels and 40 pennies are 50¢
1 nickel and 45 pennies are 50¢
50 pennies are 50¢

p. 23

36¢	51¢	76¢
+ 19¢	+ 12¢	+ 23¢
= 55¢	= 63¢	= 99¢

pp. 26–27

50¢	73¢	25¢
− 29¢	− 67¢	− 19¢
= 21¢	= 6¢	= 6¢

Text copyright © 2017 by David A. Adler
Illustrations copyright © 2017 by Edward Miller
All Rights Reserved
HOLIDAY HOUSE is registered in the U.S. Patent and Trademark Office.
Printed and bound in March 2017 at Toppan Leefung, DongGuan City, China.
The artwork was created on the computer.
www.holidayhouse.com
First Edition
1 3 5 7 9 10 8 6 4 2

Library of Congress Cataloging-in-Publication Data

Names: Adler, David A. | Miller, Edward, 1964- illustrator.
Title: Money math : addition and subtraction / by David A. Adler ;
illustrated by Edward Miller. First edition.
Description: New York : Holiday House, 2017. | Audience: Age 5–8. |
Audience: K to grade 3.
Identifiers: LCCN 2016050864 | ISBN 9780823436989 (hardcover)
Subjects: LCSH: Addition—Juvenile literature. | Subtraction—Juvenile
literature. | Money—United States—Juvenile literature.
Classification: LCC QA115 .A3655 2017 | DDC 513.2/11—dc23
LC record available at https://lccn.loc.gov/2016050864

Visit www.davidaadler.com for more information on the author, a list of his books, and
teacher's guides and educational materials. You can also learn more about the writing
process, take fun quizzes, and read selected pages from David A. Adler's books.

Visit Edward Miller on Facebook at Edward Elementary.